1 MONTH OF
FREE
READING

at
www.ForgottenBooks.com

By purchasing this book you are eligible for one month membership to ForgottenBooks.com, giving you unlimited access to our entire collection of over 1,000,000 titles via our web site and mobile apps.

To claim your free month visit:

www.forgottenbooks.com/free902511

ISBN 978-0-266-87252-8
PIBN 10902511

For support please visit www.forgottenbooks.com

1861.

THE KNOX

Fruit Farm and Nurseries

Strawberries, Raspberries, Blackberries,

Grapes, Currants, Gooseberries, &c., &c.

POST OFFICE ADDRESS:

J. KNOX, BOX 155, PITTSBURGH, PA.

S

C

1861.

CATALOGUE

OF

STRAWBERRIES,

RASPBERRIES, BLACKBERRIES,

Currants, Gooseberries, Grapes, &c.

CULTIVATED BY

J. KNOX,

KNOX FRUIT FARM AND NURSERIES.

POST OFFICE ADDRESS:

J. KNOX, BOX 155, PITTSBURGH, PA.

THE KNOX FRUIT FARM.

In presenting our Catalogue of "Small Fruits," for the
Spring of 1861, we take the liberty of inserting an article
descriptive of our place, published in the Pittsburgh Even-
ing Chronicle last Summer, and written by the Editor,
CHARLES McKNIGHT, ESQ. The article gives, to some extent, our choice of varieties, as well as some information
in regard to our mode of culture.

A VISIT TO KNOX'S SMALL FRUIT FARM.
100 ACRES IN FRUIT; 50 ACRES IN STRAWBERRIES.

Having long heard of, and desired to see the "Small
Fruit" Farm of REV. J. KNOX, we took advantage the other day of a leisure afternoon to pay it a visit. We were so
much pleased and astonished at what we saw, that we feel
prompted to give our readers a somewhat extended descrip-
tion of it. This extensive and highly cultivated farm is a
credit to Pittsburgh, and Mr. Knox deserves most honora-
ble mention for the enterprise and perseverance which has
induced him to increase, year by year, his plantation of
"Small Fruits," until now they are beyond any peradven-
ture, not only the lragest and most complete of any in the
West, but of any in the United States. If, as has been

well said, that man should be esteemed a public benefactor who causes two blades of grass to grow where but one grew before, how much more he who devotes his whole time and means to the culture, improvement and multiplication of various kinds of the most delicious fruit; who supplies not only our own, but far distant and diverse markets, with such abundance and superior qualities of berries, as but a few years ago would have been considered unattainable. Nothing in the art of horticulture, arbiculture, or floriculture, is, to our minds, more instructive or interesting, than to witness the almost endless varieties which have, by progressive and experimental culture, been produced from one parent stock. For example, the wonderful varieties of multiform and varicolored roses, which are now catalogued by the florist or nurseryman, are but the result of science and culture applied to the improvement of the common wild rose of our forests. So almost innumerable varieties of apples, peaches, plums, grapes, strawberries, and more lately of blackberries, can all be clearly and unerringly traced back to a few common and inferior species. A very few years only have elapsed since any especial attention has been devoted to the last four varieties of fruit above mentioned, or what are now best known as "Small Fruits," and yet now we have almost innumerable and ever increasing varieties of them, contributing to the health and comfort of man, ministering to his tastes, and supplying him with an endless profusion of most lucious and delicious fruit. The latest products of these berries are as far superior in size, flavor, productiveness, and profitableness to those brought to our markets but a few years since, as the splendid Tube, or Monthly roses, are to their original—the modest and humble native of the forest, for as the Golden Gate and Newton Pippin are to the sour and forbidding Crab, which contracts the mouth like a parsimmon. We have little doubt, too, that we have only seen the beginning of fruit culture, and that those which are now considered the best and most delicious kinds of fruits, will be discarded for such as have been produced far better and much more delicious. But we wander.

A GENERAL DESCRIPTION OF THE FARM.

The "Small Fruit" farm of Rev. J. Knox is situated on the summit, but somewhat back from the brow of Coal Hill, nearly above Birmingham, and about a mile and a half distant from the city. The farm comprises one hundred and twenty-five acres, fully one hundred of which is in close and unintermittent cultivation; the rest is occupied by vegetables, gardens, dwellings, out-houses, woods, &c., &c.— The mansion, which is poised nearly in the centre of the ground, is a plain, but roomy and comfortable structure, of two stories, and surrounded by a broad porch. It looks very much like one of those commodious planter's houses, which are so often met with in the cotton states. This farm of one hundred acres is quite equivalent—so careful is the mode of culture, and such the economy of space and growths—to a farm double the size. As an instance of how economy of space and time is regarded, we saw in one division, a thrifty young peach orchard, of some ten acres extent, the trees of which were not expected to produce for four years. To turn this soil and time to profit until the trees commenced to yield their golden fruitage, Mr. Knox had planted out between each row of trees, a line of Black Cap raspberries, which would be profitable for fruit and plants for four years, and between each row of trees, at right angles to the other rows, a line of strawberries, from which he expected three crops of fruit and plants, so that while the trees were unproductive, the other crops would be highly remunerative, and when the trees commenced bearing, and needed all the soil's nourishment, the "Small Fruit" plantations would have served their ends, and would be ready for rooting up.

The entire farm is divided about thus—fifty acres in strawberries, ten in raspberries, ten in blackberries, seventeen in peaches, ten in apples, and three in very select varieties of the grape, chiefly the Concord, Delaware and Diana, raised for fruit, for wine making, and for propagating. We need not dwell on the apple or peach orchards—although Mr. Knox is one of the best and most successful pomologists, and has as choice a selection as any in the country—nor on the graperies, or their peculiar mode of culture; nor on the large and highly profitable patches of choice currents, goose-berry, and giant rhubarb, cultivated for the market and for wine making. These, while they engage close attention, and most approved culture, are not Mr, Knox's specialities; but let us rather regard and describe the Strawberry, Raspberry and Blackberry divisions of the grounds. We should first premise, however, that Mr. Knox's business is two-fold—to cultivate these berries for market, aad to propagate plants for sale. In both of these branches he has been already highly successful. His plants of every variety of these three berries have been transmitted, carefully packed, to every State South and West of us, while his berries have found a ready market, and at the highest prices, not only at home, but abroad.

MR. KNOX'S PECULIAR MODE OF CULTURE.

It may not be, though it should be, known to all our readers, that Pittsburgh has the reputation of producing the largest, if not the most delicious and finest-flavored strawberries in the United States, and frequently has Mr, Knox's salesman furnished an admiring New Yorker, or Philadelphian, visiting our markets, a quart box of his strawberries for a dollar per box, to be sent on East as samples of remarkable size and superior excellence. This superiority in our berries is greatly owing, at least with Mr. Knox, to his peculiar and unusually careful and expensive mode of culture. Where large tracts of berries are grown, the plants, or bushes, are usually allowed to run together, and closely occupy the whole field—not so at this farm. They are all set in perfectly straight and equidistant rows. The ground is frequently and abundantly enriched after the most approved treatment. The soil is often, and very thoroughly stirred by suitable cultivators, by the hoe, and otherwise, and then gone over at regular intervals and throughout the year, by hand. Every weed is rooted out; every plant examined, and every thing removed which might prove noxious, or added which might prove beneficial to the plant's health, thriftiness and productiveness. This very laborious and expensive culture, would be considered by most fruitists ridiculous and unprofitable, but Mr. Knox thinks—nay, he knows, that it pays, and that very largely. The·more he has tried, and experienced their benefits, the more does he resolve to continue his care and minute labors. For this elaborate culture and manipulation, a very large force is requisite, and in spring time, when the plants are putting forth their green leaves, and when every attention tells directly on the fruit, *over one hundred persons are employed on the yrounds at one time.* But let us proceed at once to the

STRAWBERRY PLANTATIONS,

Comprising fully fifty acres, forty of which were planted out this Spring. They are divided into specimen, fruiting and propagating beds, In the specimen bed, there is grown a single row of most of the varieties known—and each kept perfectly distinct by the constant removal of runners. Such a bed is of manifest advantage in affording visitors opportunity to examine and compare in close proximity, the plants and fruit of a large collection. The propagation beds are for the production of new plants, by their parent plants being allowed to make runners and strike out roots. The different varieties are grown so remote from each other, and are numbered and registered with such care, as to preclude all possibility of any admixture of sorts. The fruit beds are, as mentioned above, planted and cultivated in rows, no runner being allowed io extend or root itself. This is garden culture introduced into the field. So far as we know, Mr. Knox is the only person in the country who has adopted this expensive and elaborate mode of culture on a large scale, and his conclusion is that it will pay better than any other treatment; that one acre thus cultivated, will produce more than five treated in the ordinary way, and that all judicious labor spent on the strawberry will pay at least one hundred per cent. Mr. Knox has in cultivation, over

one hundred varieties, some of which are but of little com-
parative value for their fruit, but which, in a general collection, are very important, as allowing persons interested to
form a correct judgment with reference to them, as well as
to compare them with others of better repute. Hence, old
and new, native and foreign, rejected and accepted varieties
have been procured, but many of them are only kept in the
specimen bed.

THE VARIOUS KINDS OF STRAWBERRIES.

The truit plantations are composed chiefly, at present, of
of the following popular varieties :—British Queen, Buist's
Prize, Boston Pine, Brighton Pine, Baltimore Scarlet, Burr's
New Pine, Compte de Flanders, Hovey's Seedling, Hooker, Honneur de Belique, Jenny Lind, Kitly's Goliath, Large
Early Scarlet, Longworth's Prolific, McAvoy's Superior,
Moyamensing, Nimrod, Peabody's Seedling, Princess Royal,
Scarlet Magnate, Scott's Seedling, Triomphe de Gand, Trollope's Victoria, Vicomptesse Herricart de Theury, and Wilson's Albany. There are about twenty-five varieties, which,
for fruit, Mr. Knox says he could not get along without,
although from three to six kinds will furnish sufficient variety for such as cultivate for family use. He regards the
Wilson's Albany as a very valuable and profitable variety,
and has shown his faith in it, by planting full fifteen acres
of it this spring. In addition to its many other excellen-
cies, it has proven a superior berry for canning, or preserving, and was this season in grat demand for these purposes.
Its weight, size, solidity, flavor and color, render it popular
for this use. It is, moreover, eminently productive, and
highly profitable as a market fruit. Mr. Knox is also very
partial to Trollope's Victoria, an excellent variety of very
large size, and delicious flavor, and which continues in bearing a long time. He has raised specimens of fruit this sea-
son, without any extra attention, measuring from $1\frac{3}{4}$ to $2\frac{1}{4}$
inches in diameter.

THE TRIOMPHE DE GAND STRAWBERRY.

But after a trial of three years, Mr. Knox placed at the head of the list of strawberries, the Triomphe de Gand. But little has yet been said about this variety, and it has not been generally cultivated, but as soon as well-known, it will be the most popular strawberry in the country. There is no known excellence which it does not possess. The plants are thrifty, hardy, and vigorous growers, bearing their fruit well up, which renders it easy to be kept clean. They are also wonderfully productive, and the fruit is not only usually of very large size, but uniformly so, and throughout the season, which is longer with it than with most other varieties. The flavor is everything which could be desired. It is of a very beautiful crimson color, glossy and alltogether lovely. It keeps well after being picked, retaining its beautiful color and firmness, and carries better than any other variety. Mr. Knox planted of this variety, last spring, four acres for fruiting, but was so well pleased with the season's crop, that he concluded to devote all of these to propagation, and will have millions of plants for sale the coming spring. Fruit of this variety, and Throllope's Victoria, was bought at Mr. Knox's Market st. stand this season, at from 50 cents to $1 per quart, and was sent to Cincinnati, Philadelphia and New York. Besides the kinds above mentioned, there is a number of foreign varieties under cultivation, that promise well. Some of them bore fruit this season of a remarkable size and beauty; but Mr. Knox wishes to test them another season, before expressing an opinion as to their value.

THE RASPBERRY DEPARTMENT,

Is as yet somwhat small when compared with his strawberry patch, but very large when considered by itself. He has ten acres, very densely planted with over twenty varieties. The Fastolff, Red Antwerp, and Hudson River Antwerp, do exceedingly well with him, but his three favorite varieties are, Brinckle's Orange, Franconia, and Improved American Black Cap. Brinckle's Orange, Mr. Knox considers the finest flavored raspberry in the world—of large size, beautiful color, unvarying productiveness, and delicious flavor. The Franconia berry is not so highly flavored, but is very large. Its size and color render it attractive, and ever procure for it a ready market. It is enormously productive, and continues a long time in bearing. The Improved American Black Cap is much superior to the common Black Cap. The fruit is sweet and juicy, and very large—sometimes measuring three quarters of an inch in diameter. Many persons prefer this to all other varieties. One advantage it possesses over all others, is its hardiness, it never requiring any winter protection. Mr. K. was so much pleased with this variety, and the fruit was found to be so popular in market this season, that he is producing, as rapidly as possible, new plants for sale, and will have a very large supply for his customers this Autumn.

THE NEW ROCHELLE BLACKBERRY.

The Blackberry patches will immediately attract the attention, and will command the marked admiration of every visitor to Mr. Knox's farm. The blackberry is a fruit which has been in culture but a very few years, but so many and so excellent have been the varieties already produced, and so enormous and profitable has proved their yield, that it is destined to become a great and indispensable favorite with both the amateur and the professional fruitist. Mr. K. has about ten acres of them in cultivation, and is rapidly increasing his plantations. The three chief varieties are the New Rochelle, the Dorchester, and the Thornless; but he esteems the Rochelle the best. Mr. K. was the first to introduce it into this market, and after overcoming many obstacles, and encountering and conquering many prejudices, he is now highly successful with it; not only sending enormous quantities of the berry to market, where it always commands from twenty to fifty cents per quart, but distributing throughout the West and South, prodigious numbers of the plants, carefully packed in tidy bundles, and imbedded in soft moss. He has now cultivated it for five years, and was highly pleased with it from the time it commenced to bear, but he thinks far more highly of it now than ever. It is in the most lively demand, not only for the fruit to eat, but for making into jams, jellies and wine, for which purpose there are none of its species can begin to compare with it.

For propagating new plants, it is also highly profitable, as it spreads with amazing rapidity, and requires but little or no care, and plants are in demand at high prices. For wine purposes it has been found, by actual experiment, to be more profitable than to sell it as edible fruit at twenty-five cents per quart. Eight gallons of berries will easily produce five gallons of rich juice, which will work well and make most delicious wine. This berry can be devoted to so many profitable purposes, that it will be found difficult to overstock the market for many years to come. Its medicinal qualities are by no means its least recommendation. During the hot season, no fruit is so grateful to the taste, or so beneficial in its influences.

In a word, it may be called the *Queen of Berries*, and Mr. Knox deserves the highest credit for enterprise in introcing this super-excellent fruit to our market, as well as doing all he possibly can to extend the culture of the berry throughout the west. It has been pronounced by many who have committed serious blunders in planting, or have tasted the fruit when not fully ripe, to be a humbug; but we have the very best evidence, and the most reliable authorities for saying, that when perfectly ripe, it is a paragon of excellence—of the most exquisite flavor, and not equalled by any berry yet grown, in beauty, size and enormous productiveness. It is by no means fully ripe when quite black. After becoming black, it tastes quite tart, and comparatively juiceless and flavorless, but if allowed to remain until just as it were melting away from the stem, it has then acquired all its richest and most savory juices, has an incomparable flavor, and is of most delicious lusciousness.

PRESENT APPEARANCE OF THE ROCHELLE.

Mr. Knox's new Rochelle plantations are now in high season. The berries are either fully ripe, or rapidly ripening, and present a sight worth going a great way to behold. We stood in the midst of a patch, and on all sides of us, stood thrifty and vigirous bushes, ladened down to the very earth, and lying along upon the ground, with large clusters of most beautiful and most appetizing fruit. Some of the bushes we saw must each of them have had from two to three dollars worth of ripe, or ripening berries upon them. We had only to take our position anywhere, stretch forth our hands, and pluck our fill of such beautiful, large, and deliciously melting berries, as we have never seen equalled, and never expect to see excelled. It makes the mouth water even to write of them. Large as these berries are, they contain scarcely any seed, but just melt away in the mouth like snow-flakes. No, the Rochelle Blakberry is no humbug, a fact most abundantly proved by those who have grown it largest and most extensively, and who now universally and enthusiastically unite in expressing their opinion that *no more productive, delicious, or profitable berry has ever yet been produced.*

THE ROCHELLE BERRY AS A WINE MAKER.

Wonders are now related of the almost incredible profit to be derived from the new Rochelle Blackberry, when expressed into wine. The largest growers are bestowing great attention to this new and valuable use for the berry. Where large markets are not accessible for the consumption of the fruit, or when the markets happen to be glutted, wine making will be its chief use. It has been proved by actual experiment, to be more remunerative to make it into wines, than to sell the fruit at twenty-five cents per quart. Its yield of wine is most generous, and the process of manufacture most simple. Eight gallons of well-ripened fruit, will yield five gallons of pure juice, to which twice the amount of water and the requisite amount of sugar is added, making fully fifteen gallons of rich, nutty, generous, and very wholesome wine.

When well made, and long enough kept, this wine has been pronounced by the very best judges, as superior to that of any native grape, excepting alone the Catawba, and in many localities, superior even to that.

SMALL FRUITS.

———————

Having for years made the cultivation of Small Fruits a specialty, and procured all the old and new varieties, both Native and Foreign, of any repute, we are now able to furnish plants in any quantity, of the best quality, and on the most reasonable terms; all of which are guaranteed to be true to name.

Great pains have been taken, not only to procure the varieties true to name, but to preserve them so. Much care is necessary to prevent the admixture of some of these fruits. But as our grounds are extensive, and we have confined our attention principally to the small fruits, and given the matter our personal supervision, we are prepared to warrant the varieties sent out as correct.

STRAWBERRIES.

We have over one hundred varieties of strawberries, and believe our collection is unsurpassed anywhere. We cordially invite the lovers of good fruit to visit our grounds when they are in bearing, and we promise to show them a display of this delicious fruit rarely to be seen. Certainly a collection embracing more than one hundred varieties of the best Foreign and Native Strawberries, is worth taking some pains to see.

Our Collection of Strawberries include:

	℔ Dozen.	℔ 100.	℔ 1000.
Alice Maud,......,.....................	50	1 50	10 00
Ajax, ...	50	1 50	10 00
Admiral Dundas, ...	50	1 50	10 00
Alpine, Bush, Red,....................	25	1 00	8 00
Alpine, Bush, White,.................	25	1 00	8 00
Alpine, Wood, Red,....................	25	1 00	5 00
Alpine, Wood, White,................	25	1 00	5 00
British Queen, (Myatt's)	50	1 50	10 00
Buist's Prize,......................	25	1 00	7 50
Boston Pine,.........................	25	1 00	7 50
Brighton Pine,......	25	1 00	7 50
Bicton Pine, (White)........,........	50	2 00	10 00
Baltimore Scarlet, (very early)......	25	1 00	7 50
Bishop's Orange,....................	25	1 00	7 50
Black Prince, ...	25	1 00	7 50
Barry's Extra,.......................	25	1 00	7 50
Belvidere	25	1 00	7 50
Boyden's Mammoth,.................	25	1 00	7 50
Brook's Prolific,....................	25	1 00	7 50
Burr's New Pine,....................	25	1 00	7 50
Burr's Seedling,..........	25	1 00	7 50
Burr's Rival Hudson,................	25	1 00	7 50
Burr's Columbus,...................	25	1 00	7 50
Burr's Scarlet Melting,.............	25	1 00	7 50
Climax,............................	25	1 00	7 50
Charles' Favorite,..................	25	1 00	7 50
Cushing,...........................	25	1 00	7 50
Cutter's Seedling, in fruit 35 days,	25	1 00	7 50
Crimson Cone,......................	25	1 00	7 50
Crystal Palace,.....................	25	1 00	7 50
Comtesse de Marne,.............	50	1 50	10 00
Comte de Flanders,..................	50	1 50	10 00
Cuthil's Black Prince,..............	50	1 50	10 00
Comte de Paris,.....................	50	1 50	10 00
Crimson Globe,..................	25	1 00	7 50
Diadem,............................	25	1 00	7 50
Dundee, .,........................	25	1 00	7 50
Duc de Brabant,.....................	50	1 50	10 00
Eclipse,............................	25	1 00	7 50
Eberline's Seedling,................	25	1 00	7 50
Filmore, (Feast's, new and fine)....	50	2 00	15 00
Genesee,...........................	25	1 00	7 50

STRAWBERRIES—Continued.

	Dozen.	100.	1000.
Globose Scarlet,	25	1 00	7 50
Golden Seeded,	50	2 00	15 00
Hovey's Seedling,	25	1 00	7 50
Hooker,	25	1 50	7 50
Hudson,	25	1 00	7 50
Harlem Orange,	25	1 00	7 50
Hooper's Seedling,	50	1 50	10 00
Honneur de la Belgique,	50	1 50	10 00
Haulbols, Prolific,	25	1 00	7 50
Iowa,	25	1 00	7 50
Imperial Scarlet,	25	1 50	7 50
Ingraham's Prince of Wales,	50	1 50	10 00
Imperial Crimson,	25	1 00	7 50
Jenny Lind,	25	1 00	7 50
Jenney's Seedling,	25	1 00	7 50
Jessee Reed,	50	2 00	15 00
Kitley's Carolina Superba,	50	2 00	15 00
Kitley's Goliath, (very large & late)	50	2 00	15 00
Large Early Scarlet,	25	1 50	7 50
Lizzie Randolph,	25	1 00	7 50
Longworth's Prolific,	25	1 50	7 50
La Rein,	25	1 50	7 50
Lady's Pine, (exquisite flavor)	25	1 00	7 50
Lucy Fitch,	25	1 00	7 50
M'Avoy's Superior,	25	1 00	7 50
M'Avoy's No. 1,	25	1 00	7 50
M'Avoy's Extra Red,	25	1 00	7 50
Moyamensing,	25	1 00	7 50
Monroe Scarlet,	25	1 00	7 50
Marylandica,	25	1 00	7 50
Marville,	25	1 00	7 50
Monstrous Swainstone,	50	2 00	10 00
Methven Castle,	25	1 00	7 50
Nimrod, (large and late)	25	1 00	7 50
Nicholson's Superb,	50	2 00	10 00
Nicholson's Filbasket,	50	2 00	10 00
Omer Pacha,	25	1 00	7 50
Ohio Mammoth,	25	1 00	7 50
Orange Prolific,	25	1 00	7 50
Peabody's Seedling,	25	1 00	7 50
Primate,	25	1 00	7 50
Palatine,	25	1 00	7 50

STRAWBERRIES—CONTINUED.

	℔ Dozen.	℔ 100.	℔ 1000.
Prince's Globose,......................	25	1 00	7 50
Premeces de Bagnoll,................	50	2 00	10 00
Princess Royal,........................	50	2 00	15 00
Reed's No. 1,...........................	25	1 00	7 50
Reed's Black Pine,...................	50	2 00	10 00
Rosalind,.................................	25	1 00	7 50
Ruby,.....................................	25	1 00	7 50
Scarlet Magnate,........................	25	1 00	7 50
Scott's Seedling,.......................	25	1 00	7 50
Scarlet Cone,...........................	25	1 00	7 50
Sir Adair,................................	25	1 00	7 50
Sir Harry, ...	25	1 00	7 50
Sterling Castle Pine,..................	25	1 00	7 50
Swainstone Seedling,..................	25	1 00	7 50
Serena, ...	25	1 00	7 50
Sireus,.	25	1 00	7 50
Schneicke's Pistillate,....	25	1 00	7 50
Triomph de Gand, (most profitable)	50	1 50	10 00
Trollope's Victoria, (large and late)	50	1 50	10 00
Tingley's Scarlet,......................	25	1 00	7 50
Vicomtesse Hericart de Thury,......	50	1 50	10 00
Victoria,..................................	25	1 00	7 50
Wilson's Albany,.......................	25	1 00	5 00

We will furnish any of the above varieties in large quantities, at greatly reduced prices.

NEW VARIETIES FOR SALE.

AUGUST AND SEPTEMBER, 1861—AND SPRING OF 1862.

Oscar, Crimson Queen, Wonderful, Wizard of the North, Austin Seedling, Downer's Prolific, Bartlett, Constance, and many others.

SELECT LIST OF STRAWBERRIES.

TEN VARIETIES, AND 1000 PLANTS FOR TEN DOLLARS.

For $10 we will furnish 100 plants each, of the following choice kinds:

Triomphe de Gand, Trollope's Victoria, Vicomtesse Hericart de Thury, Fillmore, British Queen, Burr's New Pine, Jenny Lind, Hooker, M'Avoy's Superior and Wilson's Albany.

FIVE VARIETIES, AND 500 PLANTS FOR FIVE DOLLARS.

For $5 we will furnish 100 plants each, of the following kinds:

Triomphe de Gand, Trollope's Victoria, Burr's New Pine, Jenny Lind and Wilson's Albany.

STRAWBERRY PLANTS BY MAIL.

For $1 we will send to any Post Office address in the country, postpaid, and carefully put up in cotton and oiled silk, so as to carry safely, 25 good plants of the **Wilson's Albany.** We will send, for the same price, the same number of plants (25) of any variety offered in our catalogue at 25 cents per dozen.

For $1 we will send 20 plants of the **Triomphe de Gand,** or any other variety we offer at 50 cents per dozen. No order filled for plants by mail, for less than one dollar's worth, of any one kind.

RASPBERRIES.

Our stock of plants is very large and fine. We have over twenty varieties, including

	℔ Dozen.	℔ 100.	℔ 1000
Brincle's Orange, - -	1 00	5 00	40 00
Franconia, -	1 00	4 00	35 00
Fastolff, - -	75	3 00	25 00
Rivers' Large Fruited Monthly,	75	3 00	25 00
Knevett's Giant, - -	75	3 00	25 00
Hudson River Antwerp, -	75	3 00	25 00
Red Antwerp, -	75	3 00	25 00
Yellow Antwerp, - -	75	3 00	25 00
Allen's Hardy, - -	75	3 00	25 00
Improved American Black Cap,	50	3 00	25 00

SELECT LIST OF RASPBERRIES.

For $10 we will furnish 100 **Brincle's Orange,** the finest flavored Raspberry, as well as one of the largest, most beautiful, and productive.

100 **Franconia,** a very large red berry, of good flavor, attractive, and enormously productive.

100 **Improved American Black Cap;** much larger, more juicy, better flavored, with fewer seed, and every way superior to the common Black Cap. The plant is entirely hardy and very productive, and the fruit is much sought after in the market.

The above kinds include the three colors—orange, red and black—and furnish a pleasant variety in flavor. We regard them as the best for amateurs, and the most profitable for market culture.

BLACKBERRIES.

New Rochelle,	-	1 00 per dozen;	5 00 per 100
Dorchester,	- -	75 " "	4 00 " "
Newman's Thornless,		75 " "	3 00 " "

For $10 we will send 100 of each of the above kinds.

We have fruited these varieties for five years, and having ten acres in cultivation, we are prepared to furnish wholesale purchasers at the lowest rates.

LOGAN GRAPE VINES.

Having procured a supply of the above early and valuably Grape, of A. Thomson, of Delaware, Ohio, we will furnish good, well-rooted vines, at 75 cents each—$7.00 per dozen; or by mail, securely put up, and postage paid, $1.00 each.

GRAPE VINES.

We are now propagating Grape Vines very extensively, and will have for sale in Fall of 1861, and Spring of 1862, large quantities of superior vines of

Delaware, Concord, Diana, Hartford Prolific, Anna, Herbemont, Rebecca, Elsenburg, Logan, Union Village, and others.

Currants, Gooseberries and Linnæus Rhubarb.

We will also have a large stock of *Cherry, Victoria, White Grape* and other varieties of the Currant—American Seedling Gooseberry and Linnæus Rhubarb.

ASPARAGUS ROOTS.

FOR SALE THIS SPRING.

One year,	-	50 cents per hundred
Two years,	$ 75	"
Three years,	1 00	"

TESTIMONIALS.

WILSON'S ALBANY STRAWBERRY.—This variety is still the favorite with a great many persons. Its size, enormous productiveness, and good qualities as a canning or preserving berry—weight, solidity and flavor—will continue to render it popular with buyers, and profitable for growers.

"In productiveness, it stands at the head of the list of well tried sorts."—*American Agriculturist,*

WILSON'S ALBANY has taken the lead over all other strawberries in this market the present year. They have proven much more productive than any other variety the berries of a larger and more uniform size, and of a firmer flesh, thus rendering them less liable to injury by transportation to market.—*Country Gentleman.*

"THIS is a variety that is fully worthy of the high commendations it has received, and it is decided the most prolific of any variety I ever cultivated, and the number somewhat exceed forty. It succeeds well on almost any soil, and bears abundantly. By actual measurement, it has produced with me, at the rate of 560 bushels to the acre."—*Writer in Country Gentleman.*

TRIOMPHE DE GAND STRAWBERRY.—This at present, is our favorite strawberry. For our opinion of it, please see article in front of catalogue. For all good qualities, there is no variety of which we have any knowledge, to equal it, as soon as generally known; we are satisfied it will be exceedingly popular.

Extracts from proceedings of American Pomological Society, 1860.

MILLER, of Penn'a.—" The Triomphe de Gand I have fruited for several years, and there is none which I like better for beauty, quality and productiveness."

HOPKINS.—"Have had the variety in fruit the past two years, and most cordially indorse what has been said by Mr. Miller."

BARRY.—"I consider this one of the finest strawberries in cultivation, whether native or foreign."

FULLER.—"I have several hudred varieties of strawberries, the Triomphe de Gand being one of the best."

The Standing Committee, on Foreign Fruits, of the Fruit Growers' Society, of Western New York, consistiug of Messrs. Ellwanger, T. C. Maxwell, J. C. Hanchett, C. M. Hooker, and E. A. Frost, say of the

" TRIOMPHE DE GAND—This is the finest foreign variety that has yet been tested, and there is no native variety that will compare with it in size, flavor and beauty

It is also very productive, and will doubtless prove one of the most profitable varieties for market culture."

Jenny Lind Strawberry.—*Extracts from proceedings of American Pomological Society*, 1860.

BATIHAM.—" I recommend the Jenny Lind Strawberry as worthy of general introduction."

FROST.—" This is the best Early Strawberry we have in cultivation.

QUINN.—" It is early, good and productive."

HOVEY.—" Double the size of Early Scarlet, of a good color and flavor, and productive."

PRESIDENT—" It is very popular in New England."

Improved American Black Cap Raspberry.—*Extract from President Hodge's Address before the Fruit Growers' Society, of Western New York*, 1860.

"By a scientific mode of propagating, this fruit (American Black Cap Raspberry) has not only been nearly doubled in size, but also in quantity and excellence."

Extracts from proceedings of American Pomological Society, 1860.

HOOKER.—" I propagate it for market purposes. It is different from the wild raspberry—of a far larger size, better flavored and more delicate. It is prized above all the raspberries of the season."

TROWBRIDGE.—" No other raspberry in the market brought as high a price."

NEW ROCHELLE BLACKBERRY—"Is the queen of all berries—of most magnificent proportions, exquisite flavor, and delicate texture."—*Springfield Mass. Republican.*

" A year ago it was comparatively unknown in this vicinity, until Rev. J. Knox introduced it into his garden farm. He has most successfully cultivated it, and during the fruit season last year, whole ranges of baskets of these extraordinary size and luscious fruit graced our market stands, the wonder and admiration of all, and particularly to the scientific pomologist. Every thing that Mr. Knox had claimed for this berry, has been more than realized; and through his exertions, it ranks among the very choicest of small fruits. It will be noticed that he is prepared to supply an immense number of these plants, and it may be remarked here, with great propriety, that no where else can there be furnished, such thrifty stalks, as are grown on his farm. Persons who desire the genuine plants, will profit by sending to his address for them, as there are traveling agents industriously palming off an inferior article at extravagant prices, which, in most cases, must prove a failure and disappointment wherever planted."—*Kennedy's Bank Review.*

" Having heard a good deal said about the New Rochelle Blackberry, for the past year or two, and knowing that many of the new fruits were over praised, I made a special visit, a few days since, to see for myself, and I can assure you, I was well paid for my trouble. There is no humbug about it, and the only wonder is, that it has not been more generally introduced and propagated before. The fruit is large and sweet. It is an enormous bearer; indeed, the quantity, (considering the large size of the fruit,) surprised me, and the berries were perfect."—*Chas. Downing.*

" Those who had the privilege of examining this fruit on Mr. Knox's grounds, are unanimous in their opinion that it has not been over-praised, and that in order to

be appreciated, it must be seen hanging on the plants, in its abundant, rich and beautiful clusters."—*Dr. W. Addison.*

A PROFITABLE BLACKBERRY.—The editor of the Norwalk (Ct.) *Gazette* has been
visiting the New Rochelle fields belonging to the Messrs. George Seymour & Co. and
says—" Three acres under cultivation have produced over four hundred bushels of
blackberries, with a cultivation that cost $8 per acre; and the blackberries, when sold
in New York, realized above expenses, $3,200, or more than $1000 per acre. Besides
this, thirty barrels of blackberry wine, now worth $50 per barrel, have been made
from the berries grown on the same lot; and there are plants enough for the sales
next spring, to make the net yield from this small lot, at least five thousand dollars."
—*Boston Waverly.*

" This variety of blackberry has been so long and thoroughly tried and proved,
and is so valuable, that we desire to see it everywhere introduced among our readers."
—*American Agriculturist*, October, 1859.

" We desire to have every reader of the *Agriculturist* supplied as early as possible with the luxury of a home supply of the magnificent New Rochelle Blackberry."
—*American Agriculturist*, Nov. 1859.

" The enthusiasm as to the New Rochelle Blackberry, has increased to a pro
digious extent. The quantity of this fruit sold in the New York market during the
last year, has been truly great, certainly a hundred thousand dollars' worth more
than during any former season. Perhaps no small fruit has been more profitable for
the last five years."

" One peculiarity of the New Rochelle Blackberry, is its ability to produce large
crops of fruit, even in shady positions, while its hardy, vigorous character, renders it
fit for northern cultivation, even in an exposed position."— *Working Farmer*, Janua-
ry, 1860.

" The stalks which shoot up from the roots during the summer, bear fruit the en-
suing year, and die in the autumn. This natural arrangement for reproduction, is
most beautiful. The stalks heavily laden with many hundred berries, would be exposed to the burning rays of the sun, ripen the fruit prematurely, and perish early in
the season; but being protected by new and vigorous shoots, bending gracefully like
a plume over them, continue to yield fruit daily for six or eight weeks, when the sap
being no longer elaborated, the shoot loses its vitality, and it must be removed in the
spring, to make room for the hardy shoots which are to perform the same office in
their turn."—*Amer. Phren. Journal.*

" The vines grow quite large—many of them an inch in diameter; and the fruit
hangs in clusters, in size more like very large green gage plums, than like the ordinary blackberry. The flavor is not apparently diminished by its large size, and the few
seeds is not its least recommendation. We think this berry a valuable acquisition to
our domestic fruits, and worthy of a place in every garden."—*Amer. Agriculturist.*

" I am entirely satisfied that no fruit in our market will so amply reward cultivation—and in every garden a few of these roots would supply the table with a
healthful and relishable berry, that needs only to be known to be valued everywhere."—*Prof. M. W. Jacobus, Western Theological Seminary.*

The editor of the Pittsburgh *Chronicle* gives the following notice of it:

THE NEW ROCHELLE BLACKBERRY.—Accompanied by some gentlemen from the
city, we yesterday paid a visit to the farm of Rev. J. Knox, in Lower St. Clair town-

ship; and though we had heard much of the success which had attended his culture of the New Rochelle Blackberry, and were consequently prepared to see it in a high state of perfection, we must confess that it more than met our anticipations; and that in size, yield, and flavor, it far excelled anything we had heard or read of.

The New Rochelle Blackberry was first introduced here by Mr. Knox. He put down but a few plants at first, but their immense yield, and the superior quality of the berry, convinced him that it was just the thing for this district; and the following year, at a very great outlay, he set several acres of the plants. The result is easily told. Coming up to his warmest anticipations, he is now able to supply our market with this very desirable and beautiful berry, in large quantities; and at a time, too, when Strawberries are not to be had, and Raspberries are out of date.

The blackberries grown by Mr. Knox, are nearly as large as Plums, unusually sweet and palatable, and hang in most bountiful profusion on the bushes. On one small vine alone, there were some six hundred berries—some green, others red, more almost ripe, and not a few fit for gathering. They begin to ripen early in July, and continue in season six or seven weeks, thus furnishing us a delicious substitute for the Strawberry and the Raspberry, to either of which they are not a whit inferior. They are said to be admirably adapted for preserves, and make excellent wine—their juicy nature rendering them in this latter particular, unusually productive. They have become a great favorite in the market; and as the plant is an exceedingly hardy one, and a heavy producer, we do not see why every man possessed of a piece of ground, should not have his "New Rochelle Blackberry patch." It would furnish him a delicious berry in the season, and the surplus he might send to market, where they will ever command a remunerative price.

We have abundance of other testimony of a like character, and could say even more in its praise than we have; but let every one who has a piece of ground, if only large enough for a single plant, try it for himself, and he will be amply repaid.

☞ For other information in reference to varieties and culture, please read article in front of catalogue.